SEXUALITY IN THE AETIOLOGY OF THE NEUROSES

BY

SIGMUND FREUD

British Library Cataloguing-in-Publication Data
A catalogue record for this book is available from the
British Library

Contents

Sigmund Freud

Sigismund Schlomo Freud was born on 6th May 1856, in the Moravian town of Příbor, now part of the Czech Republic.

Sigmund was the eldest of eight children to Jewish Galician parents, Jacob and Amalia Freud. After Freud's father lost his business as a result of the Panic of 1857, the family were forced to move to Leipzig and then Vienna to avoid poverty. It was in Vienna that the nine-year-old Sigmund enrolled at the Leopoldstädter Kommunal-Realgymnasium before beginning his medical training at the University of Vienna in 1873, at the age of just 17. He studied a variety of subjects, including philosophy, physiology, and zoology, graduating with an MD in 1881.

The following year, Freud began his medical career in Theodor Meynert's psychiatric clinic at the Vienna General Hospital. He worked there until 1886 when he set up in private practice and began specialising in "nervous disorders". In the same year he married Merth Bernays, with whom he had 6 children between 1887 and 1895.

In the period between 1896 and 1901, Freud isolated himself from his colleagues and began work on developing the basics of his psychoanalytic theory. He published *The Interpretation of Dreams*, in 1899, to a lacklustre reception, but continued to produce works such as *The Psychopathology of Everyday Life* (1901) and *Three Essays on the Theory of Sexuality* (1905). He held a weekly meeting at his home known as the "Wednesday Psychological Society" which eventually developed into the Vienna Psycho-Analytic Society. His ideas gained momentum and by the end of the decade his methods were being used internationally by neurologists and psychiatrists.

Freud made a huge and lasting contribution to the field of psychology with many of his methods still being used in modern psychoanalysis. He inspired much discussion on the wealth of theories he produced and the reactions to his works began a century of great psychological investigation.

In 1930 Freud fled Vienna due to rise of Nazism and resided in England until his death from mouth cancer on 23rd September 1939.

SEXUALITY IN THE AETIOLOGY
OF THE NEUROSES
(1898)

Exhaustive researches during the last few years have led me to recognize that the most immediate and, for practical purposes, the most significant causes of every case of neurotic illness are to be found in factors arising from sexual life. This theory is not entirely new. A certain amount of importance has been allowed to sexual factors in the aetiology of the neuroses from time immemorial and by every writer on the subject. In certain marginal regions of medicine a cure for 'sexual complaints' and for 'nervous weakness' has always been promised in the same breath. When once the validity of the theory ceases to be denied, therefore, it will not be hard to dispute its originality.

In a few short papers which have appeared during the last years in the *Neurologisches Zentralblatt*, the *Revue Neurolgique* and the *Wiener klinische Rundschau*, I have tried to give an indication of the material and the points of view which offer scientific support for the theory of the 'sexual aetiology of the neuroses'. A full presentation is, however, still wanting, mainly because, in endeavouring to throw light on what is recognized as the actual state of affairs, we come upon ever fresh problems for the solution of which the necessary preliminary work has not been done. It does not seem to me at all premature, however, to attempt to direct the attention of medical practitioners to what I believe to be the facts so that they may convince themselves of the truth of my assertions and at the same time of the benefits they may derive in their practice from a knowledge of them.

I am aware that efforts will be made, by the use of arguments with an ethical colouring, to prevent the physician from pursuing the matter further. Anyone who wants to make certain whether or not his patients' neuroses are really connected with their sexual life cannot avoid asking them about their sexual life and insisting upon receiving a true account of it. But in this, it is asserted, lies the danger both for the individual and society. A doctor, I hear it being said, has no right to intrude upon his patients' sexual secrets and grossly injure their modesty (especially with women patients) by an interrogation of this sort. His clumsy hand can only ruin family happiness, offend the innocence of young people and encroach upon the authority of parents; and where adults are concerned he will come to share uncomfortable knowledge and destroy his own relations to his patients. It is therefore his ethical duty, the conclusion is, to keep away from the whole business of sex.

To this one may well reply that it is the expression of a prudery which is unworthy of a physician and which inadequately conceals its weakness behind bad arguments. If factors arising out of sexual life must really be acknowledged to be causes of illness, then, for that very reason, investigation and discussion of them automatically falls within the sphere of a physician's duty. The injury to modesty of which he is guilty in this is no different and no worse, one would imagine, than when he insists on examining a woman's genital organs in order to cure a local affection - a demand on which he is pledged to insist by his medical training itself. Even now one often hears elderly women who have spent their youth in the provinces tell of how at one time they were reduced to a state of exhaustion by excessive genital haemorrhages, because they could not make up their minds to allow a doctor to see their nakedness. The educative influence which has been exercised on the public by the medical world has, in the course of one generation, so altered things that an objection of this sort is an extremely rare occurrence among the young women of to-day. If it were to occur, it would be condemned as unreasonable prudery, as modesty in the wrong place. Are we living in Turkey, a husband would ask, where all that a sick woman may show to the physician is her arm through a hole in the wall?

It is not true that interrogation of his patients and knowledge about their sexual concerns give the physician a dangerous degree of power over them. It was possible in earlier times for the same objection to be made against the uses of anaesthetics, which deprive the patient of his consciousness and of the exercise of his will and leave it to the doctor to decide whether and when he shall regain them. And yet to-day anaesthetics have become indispensable to us because they are able, better than anything else, to assist the doctor in his medical work; and among his many other serious obligations, he has taken over the responsibility for their use.

A doctor can always do harm if he is unskilful or unscrupulous, and this is no more and no less true where it is a question of investigating his patients' sexual life than it is in other things. Naturally, if someone, after an honest self-examination, feels that he does not possess the tact, seriousness and discretion which are necessary for questioning neurotic patients, and if he is aware that revelations of a sexual character would provoke lascivious thrills in him rather than scientific interest, then he will be right to avoid the topic of the aetiology of the neuroses. All we ask, in addition, is that he should also refrain from treating nervous patients.

Nor is it true that patients put insuperable obstacles in the way of an investigation into their sexual life. After some slight hesitation, adults usually adjust themselves to the situation by saying: 'After all, I'm at the doctor's; I can say anything to him.' A great many women who find it difficult enough to go through life concealing their sexual feelings, are relieved to find that with the doctor no other consideration outweighs that of their recovery, and they are grateful to him that for once they are allowed to behave quite humanly about sexual things. A dim knowledge of the overwhelming importance of sexual factors in the production of neuroses (a knowledge which I am trying to capture afresh for science) seems never to have been lost in the consciousness of laymen. How often do we witness scenes like this : A married couple, one of whom is suffering from a neurosis, comes to us for consultation. After we have made a great many introductory remarks and apologies to the effect that no conventional barriers should exist between them and the doctor who wants to be of use in such cases, and so on, we tell them that we suspect that the cause of the illness lies in the unnatural and detrimental form of sexual intercourse which they must have chosen since the wife's last confinement. We tell them that doctors do not as a rule concern themselves with such matters, but that that is reprehensible of them, even though the patients do not want to be told about things like that, etc. Thereupon one of the couple nudges the other and says: 'You see! I told you all along it would make me ill.' And the other answers: 'Well, I know, I thought so too; but what is one to do?'

In certain other circumstances, such as when one is dealing with young girls, who, after all, are systematically brought up to conceal their sexual life, one will have to be content with a very small measure of sincere response on the part of the patient. But an important consideration comes into play here namely that a doctor who is experienced in these things does not meet his patients unprepared and as a rule does not have to ask them for information but only for a confirmation of his surmises. Anyone who will follow my indications as to how to elucidate the morphology of the neuroses and translate it into aetiological terms, will need the addition of very few further admissions from his patients; in the very description of their symptoms, which they are only too ready to give, they have usually acquainted him at the same time with the sexual factors that are hidden behind.

It would be a great advantage if sick people had a better knowledge of the certainty with which a doctor is now in a position to interpret their neurotic complaints and to infer from them their operative sexual aetiology. It would undoubtedly spur such people on to abandon their secretiveness from the moment they have made up their minds to seek help for their sufferings. Moreover, it is in the interest of all of us that a higher degree of honesty about sexual things should become a duty among men and women than has hitherto been expected of them. This cannot be anything but a gain for sexual morality. In matters of sexuality we are at present, every one of us, ill or well, nothing but hypocrites. It will be all to our good if, as a result of such general honesty, a certain amount of toleration in sexual concerns should be attained.

Doctors usually take very little interest in a good many of the questions which are discussed among neuropathologists in connection with the neuroses: whether, for instance, one is justified in making a strict differentiation between hysteria and neurasthenia, whether one may distinguish hystero-neurasthenia alongside of them, whether obsessions should be classed with neurasthenia or recognized as a separate neurosis, and so on. And, indeed, such distinctions may well be a matter of indifference to a practitioner, so long as no further consequences follow from the decisions arrived at - no deeper insight and no pointers for therapeutic treatment - and so long as the patient will in every instance be sent off to a hydropathic establishment, and be told that there is nothing the matter with him. But it will be a different thing if our point of view about the causative relations between sexuality and the neuroses is adopted. Fresh interest is then aroused in the symptomatology of the different neurotic cases, and it becomes of practical importance that one should be able correctly to break down the complicated picture into its components and correctly to name them. For the morphology of the neuroses can with little difficulty be translated into aetiology and a knowledge of the latter leads on quite naturally to new indications for methods of cure.

Now the important decision we have to make - and this can be done with certainty in every instance if the symptoms are carefully assessed - is whether the case bears the characteristics of neurasthenia or of a psychoneurosis (hysteria, obsessions).(Mixed cases in which signs of neurasthenia are combined with signs of a psychoneurosis are of very frequent occurrence; but we will leave consideration of them till later.) It is only in neurasthenias that questioning the patient succeeds in disclosing the aetiological factors in his sexual life. These factors are, of course, known to him and belong to the present time, or, more properly, to the period of his life since sexual maturity (though this delimitation does not cover every case). In psychoneuroses questioning of this kind has little result. It may perhaps give us a knowledge of the factors which have to be recognized as precipitating ones, and these may or may not be connected with sexual life. If they are, they show themselves to be no different in kind from the aetiological factors of neurasthenia; that is, they entirely lack any specific relation to the causation of the psychoneurosis. And yet, in every instance, the aetiology of the psychoneuroses, too, lies in the field of sexuality. By a curious circuitous path, of which I shall speak later, it is possible to arrive at a knowledge of this aetiology and to understand why the patient was unable to tell us anything about it. For the events and influences which lie at the root of every psychoneurosis, belong, not to the present day, but to an epoch of life which is long past and which is, as it were, a prehistoric one-to the time of early childhood; and that is why the patient, too, knows nothing of them. He has - though only in a particular sense - forgotten them.

Thus, in every case of neurosis there is a sexual aetiology; but in neurasthenia it is an aetiology of a present-day kind, whereas in the psychoneuroses the factors are of an infantile nature. This is the first great contrast in the aetiology of the neuroses. 1 A second one emerges when we take account of a difference in the symptomatology of neurasthenia itself. Here, on the one hand, we find cases in which certain complaints characteristic of neurasthenia (intracranial pressure, proneness to fatigue, dyspepsia, constipation, spinal irritation, etc.) are prominent; in other cases these signs play a minor part and the clinical picture is composed of other symptoms, all of which exhibit a relation to the nuclear symptom, that of anxiety (free anxiousness, unrest, expectant anxiety, complete, rudimentary or supplementary anxiety attacks, locomotor vertigo, agoraphobia, insomnia, increased sensitivity to pain, and so on). I have left the name of neurasthenia to the first type, but have distinguished the second type as 'anxiety neurosis'; and I have given reasons for this separation in another place, where I have also taken account of the fact that as a rule both neuroses appear together. For the present purpose it is enough to emphasize that parallel to the difference in the symptoms of these two forms of illness there goes a difference in their aetiology. Neurasthenia can always be traced back to a condition of the nervous system such as is acquired by excessive masturbation or arises spontaneously from frequent emissions; anxiety neurosis regularly discloses sexual influences which have in common the factor of reservation or of incomplete satisfaction - such as coitus interruptus, abstinence together with a lively libido, so-called unconsummated excitation, and so on. In my short paper intended to introduce anxiety neurosis I put forward the formula that anxiety is always libido which has been deflected from its employment.

Where there is a case in which symptoms of neurasthenia and of anxiety neurosis are combined - where, that is, we have a mixed case - we have only to keep to our proposition, empirically arrived at, that a mingling of neuroses implies the collaboration of several aetiological factors, and we shall find our expectation confirmed in every instance. How often these aetiological factors are linked with one another organically, through the interplay of sexual processes - for instance, coitus interruptus or insufficient potency in the man, going along with masturbation - would well deserve separate discussion.

Having diagnosed a case of neurasthenic neurosis with certainty and having classified its symptoms correctly, we are in a position to translate the symptomatology into aetiology; and we may then boldly demand confirmation of our suspicions from the patient. We must not be led astray by initial denials. If we keep firmly to what we have inferred, we shall in the end conquer every resistance by emphasizing the unshakeable nature of our convictions. In this way we learn all sorts of things about the sexual life of men and women, which might well fill a useful and instructive volume; and we learn, too, to regret from every point of view that sexual science is even to-day still regarded as disreputable. Since minor deviations from a normal *vita sexualis* are much too common for us to attach any value to their discovery, we shall only allow a serious and long continued abnormality in the sexual life of a neurotic patient to carry weight as an explanation. Moreover, the idea that one might, by one's insistence, cause a patient who is psychically normal to accuse himself falsely of sexual misdemeanours - such an idea may safely be disregarded as an imaginary danger.

If one proceeds in this manner with one's patients, one also gains the conviction that, so far as the theory of the sexual aetiology of neurasthenia is concerned, there are no negative cases. In my mind, at least, the conviction has become so certain that where an interrogation has shown a negative result, I have turned this to account too for diagnostic purposes. I have told myself, that is, that such a case cannot be one of neurasthenia. In this way I have been led in several instances to assume the presence of progressive paralysis instead of neurasthenia, because I had not succeeded in establishing the fact - a fact that was necessary for my theory - that the patient indulged very freely in masturbation; and the further course of those cases later confirmed my view. In another instance the patient, who exhibited no clear organic changes, complained of intracranial pressure, headaches and dyspepsia, but countered my suspicions about his sexual life straightforwardly and with unshaken certainty; and the possibility occurred to me that he might have a latent suppuration in one of his nasal sinuses. A specialist colleague of mine confirmed this inference I had made from the negative sexual results of my interrogation, by removing the pus from the patient's antrum and relieving him of his ailments.

The appearance of there nevertheless being 'negative cases' can arise in another way as well. Sometimes an interrogation discloses the presence of a normal sexual life in a patient whose neurosis, on a superficial view, does in fact closely resemble neurasthenia or anxiety neurosis. But a more deep -going investigation regularly reveals the true state of affairs. Behind such cases, which have been taken for neurasthenia, there lies a psychoneurosis - hysteria or obsessional neurosis. Hysteria in especial, which imitates so many organic affections, can easily assume the appearance of one of the 'actual neuroses' by elevating the latter's symptoms into hysterical ones. Such hysterias in the form of neurasthenia are not even very rare. Falling back on psychoneurosis when a case of neurasthenia shows a negative sexual result, is, however, no cheap way out of the difficulty;

the proof that we are right is to be obtained by the method which alone unmasks hysteria with certainty - the method of psycho-analysis, to which we shall refer presently.

There may perhaps be some, however, who are quite willing to recognize the sexual aetiology in their neurasthenic patients, but who nevertheless blame it as one-sidedness if they are not asked to pay attention as well to the other factors which are always mentioned by the authorities as causes of neurasthenia. Now it would never occur to me to substitute a sexual aetiology in neuroses for every other aetiology, and so to assert that the latter have no operative force. This would be a misunderstanding. What I think is rather that in addition to all the familiar aetiological factors which have been recognized - and probably correctly so - by the authorities as leading to neurasthenia, the sexual factors, which have not hitherto been sufficiently appreciated, should also be taken into account. In my opinion, however, these sexual factors deserve to be given a special place in the aetiological series. For they alone are never absent in any case of neurasthenia, they alone are capable of producing the neurosis without any further assistance, so that those other factors seem to be reduced to the role of an auxiliary and supplementary aetiology, and they alone allow the physician to recognize firm relations between their manifold nature and the multiplicity of the clinical pictures. If, on the other hand, I group together all the patients who have ostensibly become neurasthenic from overwork, emotional agitation, as an after-effect of typhoid fever, and so on, they show me nothing in common in their symptoms. The nature of their aetiology gives me no idea of what kind of symptoms to expect, any more than, conversely, does the clinical picture they present enable me to infer what aetiology is at work in them.

The sexual causes, too, are the ones which most readily offer the physician a foothold for his therapeutic influence. Heredity is no doubt an important factor, when it is present; it enables a strong pathological effect to come about where otherwise only a very slight one would have resulted. But heredity is inaccessible to the physician's influence; everyone is born with his own hereditary tendencies to illness, and we can do nothing to change them. Nor should we forget that it is precisely in regard to the aetiology of the neurasthenias that we must necessarily deny the first place to heredity. Neurasthenia (in both its forms) is one of those affections which anyone may easily acquire without having any hereditary taint. If it were otherwise, the enormous increase in neurasthenia, of which all the authorities complain, would be unthinkable. In what concerns civilization, among whose sins people so often include responsibility for neurasthenia, these authorities may indeed be right (although the way in which this comes about is probably quite different from what they imagine). Yet the state of our civilization is, once again, something that is unalterable for the individual. Moreover this factor, being common to all the members of the same society, can never explain the fact of selectivity in the incidence of the illness. The physician who is not neurasthenic is exposed to the same influence of an allegedly detrimental civilization as the neurasthenic patient whom he has to treat. Subject to these limitations, the factors of exhaustion retain their significance. But the element of 'overwork', which physicians are so fond of producing to their patients as the cause of their neurosis, is too often unduly misused. It is quite true that anyone who, owing to sexual noxae, has made himself disposed to neurasthenia, tolerates intellectual work and the psychical exigencies of life badly; but no one ever becomes neurotic through work or excitement alone. Intellectual work is rather a protection against falling ill of neurasthenia; it is precisely the most unremitting intellectual workers who remain exempt from neurasthenia, and what neurasthenics complain of as 'overwork that is making them ill' does not as a rule deserve to be called 'intellectual work' at all, either in its quality or quantity. Physicians will have to become accustomed to explaining to an office-worker who has been 'overworked' at his desk or to a housewife for whom her domestic activities have become too heavy, that they have fallen ill, not because they have tried to carry out duties which are in fact easily performed by a civilized brain, but because all the while they have been grossly neglecting and damaging their sexual life.

Furthermore, it is only the sexual aetiology which makes it possible for us to understand all the details of the clinical history of neurasthenics, the mysterious improvements in the middle of the course of the illness and the equally incomprehensible deteriorations, both of which are usually related by doctors and patients to whatever treatment has been adopted. In my records, which include more than two hundred cases, there is, for instance, the story of a man who, when the treatment prescribed by his family physician had done him no good, went to Pastor Kneipp and for a year after being treated by him showed an extraordinary improvement in the middle of his illness. But when, a year later, his symptoms grew worse once more and he again went to Wörishofen for help, the second treatment was unsuccessful. A glance into the patient's family record solved the double riddle. Six and a half months after his first return from Wörishofen his wife bore him a child. This meant that he had left her at the beginning of a pregnancy of which he was not yet aware; after his return he was able to practise *natural* intercourse with her. At the close of this period, which had a curative effect on him, his neurosis was started up afresh by his once more resorting to coitus interruptus; the second treatment was bound to prove a failure, since this pregnancy of his wife's remained her last.

There was a similar case, in which, once again, the treatment had an unexpected effect which called for an explanation. This case turned out to be still more instructive, for it exhibited a puzzling alternation in the symptoms of the neurosis. A young neurotic patient had been sent by his physician to a reputable hydropathic establishment on account of a typical neurasthenia. There his condition steadily improved at first, so that there was every prospect that he would be discharged as a grateful disciple of hydrotherapy. But in the sixth week a complete change occurred; the patient 'could no longer tolerate the water', became more and more nervous, and finally left the establishment after two more weeks, uncured and dissatisfied. When he complained to me about this therapeutic fraud I asked him a few questions about the symptoms which had overtaken him in the middle of the treatment. Curiously enough, a complete change had come over them. He had *entered* the sanatorium with intracranial pressure, fatigue and dyspepsia; what had troubled him *during* the treatment were excitement, attacks of dyspnoea, vertigo in walking, and disturbances of sleep. I was now able to say to him: 'You are doing hydrotherapy an injustice. As you yourself very well knew, you fell ill as a result of long-continued masturbation. In the sanatorium you gave up this form of satisfaction, and therefore you quickly recovered. When you felt well, however, you unwisely sought to have relations with a lady

- a fellow-patient, let us suppose - which could only lead to excitement without normal satisfaction. The beautiful walks in the neighbourhood of the establishment gave you ample opportunity for this. It was this relationship, not a sudden inability to tolerate hydrotherapy, which caused you to fall ill once more. Moreover, your present state of health leads me to conclude that you are continuing this relationship here in town as well.' I can assure my readers that the patient confirmed what I said, point by point.

The present treatment of neurasthenia - which is, perhaps, carried out most successfully in hydropathic establishments - has as its aim the amelioration of the nervous condition by means of two factors : shielding the patient and strengthening him. I have nothing to say against such a method of treatment, except that it takes no account of the circumstances of the patient's sexual life. According to my experience, it is highly desirable that the medical directors of such establishments should become properly aware that they are dealing, not with victims of civilization or heredity, but - *sit venia verbo* - with people who are crippled in sexuality. They would then, on the one hand, be more easily able to account for their successes as well as their failures; and, on the other, they would achieve new successes which, till now, have been at the mercy of chance or of the patient's unguided behaviour. If we take a neurasthenic woman, suffering from anxiety, away from her home and send her to a hydropathic establishment, and if there, freed from all duties, she is made to bathe and take exercise and eat plenty of food, we shall certainly be inclined to think that the improvement - often a brilliant one - which is achieved in a few weeks or months is due to the rest which she has enjoyed and to the invigorating effects of hydrotherapy. That may be so: but we are overlooking the fact that her removal from home also entails an interruption of marital intercourse, and that it is only the temporary elimination of this pathogenic cause which makes it possible for her to recover under favourable treatment. Neglect of this aetiological point of view brings its subsequent revenge, when what seemed such a gratifying cure turns out to be a very transitory one. Soon after the patient has returned to ordinary life the symptoms of the complaint appear once more and oblige him either to spend a part of his existence unproductively from time to time in establishments of this kind or to direct his hopes of recovery elsewhere. It is therefore clear that with neurasthenia the therapeutic problems must be attacked, not in hydropathic institutions but within the framework of the patient's life.

In other cases our aetiological theory can help the physician in charge of the institution by throwing light on the source of failures which occur in the institution itself, and can suggest to him means of avoiding them. Masturbation is far commoner among grown-up girls and mature men than is generally supposed, and it has a harmful effect not only by producing neurasthenic symptoms, but also because it keeps the patients under the weight of what they feel to be a disgraceful secret. Physicians who are not accustomed to translate neurasthenia into masturbation account for the patient's pathological state by referring it to some catchword like anaemia, undernourishment, overwork, etc., and then expect to cure him by applying a therapy devised against those conditions. To their astonishment, however, periods of improvement in him alternate with periods in which all his symptoms grow worse and are accompanied by severe depression. The outcome of such a treatment is, in general, doubtful. If physicians knew that all the while the patient was struggling against his sexual habit and that he was in despair because he had once more been obliged to give way to it, if they understood how to win his secret from him, to make it less serious in his eyes and to support him in his fight against the habit, then the success of their therapeutic efforts might in this way well be assured.

To break the patient of the habit of masturbating is only one of the new therapeutic tasks which are imposed on the physician who takes the sexual aetiology of the neurosis into account; and it seems that precisely this task, like the cure of any other addiction, can only be carried out in an institution and under medical supervision. Left to himself, the masturbator is accustomed, whenever something happens that depresses him, to return to his convenient form of satisfaction. Medical treatment, in this instance, can have no other aim than to lead the neurasthenic, who has now recovered his strength, back to normal sexual intercourse. For sexual need, when once it has been aroused and has been satisfied for any length of time, can no longer be silenced; it can only be displaced along another path. Incidentally, the same thing applies to all treatments for breaking an addiction. Their success will only be an apparent one, so long as the physician contents himself with withdrawing the narcotic substance from his patients, without troubling about the source from which their imperative need for it springs. 'Habit' is a mere form of words, without any explanatory value. Not everyone who has occasion to take morphia, cocaine, chloral hydrate, and so on, for a period, acquires in this way an 'addiction' to them. Closer enquiry usually shows that these narcotics are meant to serve - directly or indirectly - as a substitute for a lack of sexual satisfaction; and whenever normal sexual life can no longer be re-established, we can count with certainty on the patient's relapse.

Another task is set to the physician by the aetiology of anxiety neurosis. It consists in inducing the patient to give up all detrimental forms of sexual intercourse and to adopt normal sexual relations. This duty, it will be understood, falls primarily on the patient's trusted physician - his family doctor; and he will do his patient a serious injury if he regards himself as too respectable to intervene in this field.

Since in these instances it is most often a question of a married couple, the physician's efforts at once encounter Malthusian plans for limiting the number of conceptions in marriage. There seems to me no doubt that such proposals are gaining ground more and more among our middle classes. I have come across some couples who have already begun practising methods for preventing conception as soon as they have had their first child, and others whose sexual intercourse was from their wedding-night designed to comply with that purpose. The problem of Malthusianism is far-reaching and complicated, and I have no intention of handling it here in the exhaustive manner which would actually be necessary for the treatment of neuroses. I shall only consider what attitude a physician who recognizes the sexual aetiology of the neuroses had best take up towards the problem.

The worst thing he can do is obviously - under whatever pretext - to try to ignore it. Nothing that is necessary can be beneath my dignity as a doctor; and it is necessary to give a married couple who contemplate limiting the number of their offspring the assistance of one's medical advice if one does not want to expose one or both of them to a neurosis. It cannot be denied that in any marriage Malthusian preventive measures will become necessary at some time or other; and, from a theoretical point of view, it would be one of the greatest triumphs of humanity, one of the most tangible liberations from the constraints of nature to which mankind is subject, if we could succeed in raising the responsible act of procreating children to the level of a deliberate and intentional activity and in freeing it from its entanglement with the necessary satisfaction of a natural need.

A perspicacious physician will therefore take it upon himself to decide under what conditions the use of measures for preventing conception are justified, and, among those measures, he will have to separate the harmful from the harmless ones. Everything is harmful that hinders the occurrence of satisfaction. But, as we know, we possess at present no method of preventing conception which fulfils every legitimate requirement - that is, which is certain and convenient, which does not diminish the sensation of pleasure during coitus and which does not wound the woman's sensibilities. This sets physicians a practical task to the solution of which they could bend their energies with rewarding results. Whoever fills in this lacuna in our medical technique will have preserved the enjoyment of life and maintained the health of numberless people; though, it is true, he will also have paved the way for a drastic change in our social conditions.

This does not exhaust the possibilities which flow from a recognition of the sexual aetiology of the neuroses. The main benefit which we obtain from it for neurasthenics lies in the sphere of prophylaxis. If masturbation is the cause of neurasthenia in youth, and if, later on, it acquires aetiological significance for anxiety neurosis as well, by reason of the reduction of potency which it brings about, then the prevention of masturbation in both sexes is a task that deserves more attention than it has hitherto received. When we reflect upon all the injuries, both the grosser and the finer ones, which proceed from neurasthenia - a disorder which we are told is growing more and more prevalent - we see that it is positively a matter of public interest that *men should enter upon sexual relations with full potency*. In matters of prophylaxis, however, the individual is relatively helpless. The whole community must become interested in the matter and give their assent to the creation of generally acceptable regulations. At present we are still far removed from such a state of affairs which would promise relief, and it is for this reason that we may with justice regard civilization, too, as responsible for the spread of neurasthenia. Much would have to be changed. The resistance of a generation of physicians who can no longer remember their own youth must be broken down; the pride of fathers, who are unwilling to descend to the level of humanity in their children's eyes, must be overcome; and the unreasonable prudery of mothers must be combated - the mothers who at present look upon it as an incomprehensible and undeserved stroke of fate that '*their* children should have been the ones to become neurotic'. But above all, a place must be created in public opinion for the discussion of the problems of sexual life. It will have to become possible to talk about these things without being stamped as a trouble-maker or as a person who makes capital out of the lower instincts. And so here, too, there is enough work left to do for the next hundred years - in which our civilization will have to learn to come to terms with the claims of our sexuality.

The value of making a correct diagnostic separation of the psychoneuroses from neurasthenia is also shown by the fact that the psychoneuroses call for a different practical assessment and for special therapeutic measures. They make their appearance as a result of two kinds of determinants, either independently or in the train of the 'actual neuroses' (neurasthenia and anxiety neurosis). In the latter case we are dealing with a new type of neurosis - incidentally, a very frequent one - a mixed neurosis. The aetiology of the 'actual neuroses' has become an auxiliary aetiology of the psychoneuroses. A clinical picture arises in which, let us say, anxiety neurosis predominates but which also contains traits of genuine neurasthenia, hysteria and obsessional neurosis. When confronted with a mixture of this kind, we shall nevertheless not be wise to give up separating out the clinical pictures proper to each neurotic illness; for after all it is not difficult to explain the case to oneself in the following manner. The predominant place taken by the anxiety neurosis shows that the illness has come into being under the aetiological influence of an 'actual' sexual noxa. But the person concerned was, apart from that, disposed to one or more of the psychoneuroses owing to a special aetiology and would at some time or other have fallen ill of a psychoneurosis either spontaneously or with the advent of some other weakening factor. In this way the auxiliary aetiology for the psychoneurosis which is still lacking is supplied by the actual aetiology of the anxiety neurosis.

For such cases it has quite correctly come to be the therapeutic practice to disregard the psychoneurotic components in the clinical picture and to treat the 'actual neurosis' exclusively. In very many cases it is possible to overcome the neurosis as well which it has brought along with it, provided that the neurasthenia is effectively dealt with. But a different view must be taken in those cases of psychoneurosis which either appear spontaneously or remain behind as an independent entity after an illness composed of neurasthenia and psychoneurosis has run its course. When I speak of a 'spontaneous' appearance of a psychoneurosis, I do not mean that anamnestic investigation shows us no aetiological element whatever. It may do so, no doubt; but it may also happen that our attention is directed to some indifferent factor - an emotional state, an enfeeblement owing to physical illness, and so on. It must, however, be borne in mind in all these cases that the true aetiology of the psychoneuroses does not lie in such precipitating causes, but remains beyond the reach of ordinary anamnestic examination.

As we know, it is in an attempt to bridge this gap that the assumption has been made of a special neuropathic disposition (which, incidentally, if it existed, would not leave much hope of success for the treatment of such pathological conditions). The neuropathic disposition itself is regarded as a sign of a general degeneracy, and thus this convenient technical term has come to be superabundantly used against the wretched patients whom the doctors are quite incapable of helping. Fortunately, the state of affairs is different. The neuropathic disposition does no doubt exist, but I must deny that it suffices for the creation of a psychoneurosis. I must further deny that the conjunction of a neuropathic disposition with precipitating causes occurring in later life constitutes an adequate aetiology of the psychoneuroses. In tracing back the vicissitudes of an individual's illness to the experiences of his ancestors, we have gone too far; we have forgotten that between his conception and his maturity there lies a long and important period of life - his childhood - in which the seeds of later illness may be acquired. And that- is what in fact happens with a psychoneurosis. Its true aetiology is to be found in childhood experiences, and, once again - and exclusively - in impressions concerned with sexual life. We do wrong to ignore the sexual life of children entirely; in my experience, children are capable of every psychical sexual activity, and many somatic sexual ones as well. Just as the whole human sexual apparatus is not comprised in the external genitals and the two reproductive glands, so human sexual life does not begin only with puberty, as on a rough inspection it may appear to do. Nevertheless it is true that the organization and evolution of the human species strives to avoid any great degree of sexual activity during childhood. It seems that in man the sexual instinctual forces are meant to be stored up so that, on their release at puberty, they may serve great cultural ends. (W. Fliess.) Consideration of this sort may make it possible to understand why the sexual experiences of childhood are bound to have a pathogenic effect. But they produce their effect only to a very slight degree at the time at which they occur; what is far more important is their *deferred* effect, which can only take place at later periods of growth. This deferred effect originates - as it can do in no other way - in the psychical traces which have been left behind by infantile sexual experiences. During the interval between the experiences of those impressions and their reproduction (or rather, the reinforcement of the libidinal impulses which proceed from them), not only the somatic sexual apparatus but the psychical apparatus as well has undergone an important development; and thus it is that the influence of these earlier sexual experiences now leads to an abnormal psychical reaction, and psychopathological structures come into existence.

I can do no more in these brief hints than mention the chief factors on which the theory of the psychoneuroses is based: the deferred nature of the effect and the infantile state of the sexual apparatus and of the mental instrument. To reach a true understanding of the mechanism by which the psychoneuroses come about, a more extended exposition would be necessary. Above all, it would be indispensable to put forward as worthy of belief certain hypotheses, which seem to me to be new, about the composition and mode of operation of the psychical apparatus. In a book on the interpretation of dreams on which I am now engaged I shall find occasion to touch upon those fundamental elements of a psychology of the neuroses. For dreams belong to the same set of psychopathological structures as hysterical *idées fixes*, obsessions, and delusions.

Since the manifestations of the psychoneuroses arise from the deferred action of unconscious psychical traces, they are accessible to psychotherapy. But in this case the therapy must pursue paths other than the only one so far followed of suggestion with or without hypnosis. Basing myself on the 'cathartic' method introduced by Josef Breuer, I have in recent years almost completely worked out a therapeutic procedure which I propose to describe as '*psycho-analytic*'. I owe a great number of successes to it, and I hope I may be able further to increase it effectiveness considerably. The first accounts of the technique and scope of this method were given in *Studies on*

Hysteria, written jointly with Breuer and published in 1895. Since then a good deal, as I think I may say, has been altered for the better. Whereas at that time we modestly declared that we could undertake to only to remove the symptoms of hysteria, not to cure hysteria itself, this distinction has since come to seem to me without substance, so that there is a prospect of a genuine cure of hysteria and obsessions. It is therefore with very lively interest that I have read in the publications of colleagues that 'in this case the ingenious procedure devised by Breuer and Freud has failed', or that 'the method has not performed what it seemed to promise'. This gave me something of the feelings of a man who reads his own obituary in the paper, but who is able to reassure himself by his better knowledge of the facts. For the method is so difficult that it has quite definitely to be learned; and I cannot recall that a single one of my critics has expressed a wish to learn it from me. Nor do I believe that, like me, they have occupied themselves with it intensely enough to have been able to discover it for themselves. The remarks in the *Studies on Hysteria* are totally inadequate to enable a reader to master the technique, nor are they in any way intended to give any such complete instruction.

Psycho-analytic therapy is not at present applicable to all cases. It has, to my knowledge, the following limitations. It demands a certain degree of maturity and understanding in the patient and is therefore not suited for the young or for adults who are feeble-minded or uneducated. It also fails with people who are very advanced in years, because, owing to the accumulation of material in them, it would take up so much time that by the end of the treatment they would have reached a period of life in which value is no longer attached to nervous health. Finally, the treatment is only possible if the patient has a normal psychical state from which the pathological material can be mastered from which to work ie a relatively normal ego. During a condition of hysterical confusion, or an interpolated mania or melancholia, nothing can be effected by psycho-analytic means. Such cases can nevertheless be treated by analysis after the violent manifestations have been quieted by the usual measures. In actual practice, chronic cases of psychoneurosis are altogether more amenable to the method than cases with acute crises, in which the greatest stress is naturally laid on the speed with which the crises can be dealt with. For this reason, the most favourable field of work for this new therapy is offered by hysterical phobias and the various forms of obsessional neurosis.

That the method is confined within these limits is to a large extent explained by the circumstances in which I had to work it out. My material does in fact consist of chronic nervous cases derived from the more educated classes. I think it very probable that supplementary methods may be devised for treating children and the public who go for assistance to hospitals. I ought also to say that up to the present I have tried my treatment exclusively on *severe* cases of hysteria and obsessional neurosis; I cannot tell how it would turn out with those mild cases which, to all appearance at least, are cured by some unspecific kind of treatment lasting for a few months. It will readily be understood that a new therapy which calls for many sacrifices can only reckon on obtaining patients who have already tried the generally accepted methods without success, or whose condition has justified the inference that they could expect nothing from these supposedly more convenient and shorter therapeutic procedures. Thus it happened that I was obliged to tackle the hardest tasks straightaway with an imperfect instrument. The test has proved all the more convincing.

The main difficulties which still stand in the way of the psycho-analytic method of cure. It is no more than a necessary corollary to this complete ignorance that doctors consider themselves justified in using the most unfounded assurances for the consolation of their patients or in order to induce them to adopt therapeutic measures. 'Come to my sanatorium for six weeks', they will say, 'and you will get rid of your symptoms' (travel anxiety, obsessions, and so on).Sanatoria are, it is true, indispensable for calming acute attacks that may arise in the course of a psychoneurosis by diverting the patient's attention, nursing him and taking care of him. But towards removing chronic conditions they achieve precisely nothing: and the superior sanatoria, which are supposed to be conducted on scientific lines, do no more than the ordinary hydropathic establishments.

It would be more dignified as well as more helpful to the patient - who, after all, has to come to terms with his ailments - for the doctor to tell the truth, as he knows it from his daily practice. The psychoneuroses as a genus are by no means mild illnesses. When hysteria sets in, no one can foretell when it will come to an end. We mostly comfort ourselves with the vain prophecy that 'one day it will suddenly disappear'. Recovery often enough turns out to be merely an agreement to mutual toleration between the sick part of the patient and the healthy part; or it is the result of the transformation of a symptom into a phobia. A girl's hysteria, calmed down with difficulty, revives in her as a wife after the short interruption of young married happiness. The only difference is that another person, the husband, is now driven by his own interests to keep silence about her condition. Even if an illness of this kind leads to no manifest incapacity on the patients' part to carry on their life, it nearly always prevents free unfolding of their mental powers. Obsessions recur throughout their lives; and phobias and other restrictions upon the will have hitherto been unamenable to treatment of any kind. All this is kept from the knowledge of the layman. The father of a hysterical girl is consequently horrified if, for instance, he is asked to agree to her being given a year's treatment, when she has perhaps only been ill for a few months. The layman is, as it were, deeply convinced in himself that all these psychoneuroses are unnecessary; so he has no patience with the processes of the illness and no readiness to make sacrifices for its treatment. If, in face of a case of typhus which lasts three weeks, or of a broken leg which takes six months to mend, he adopts a more understanding attitude, and if, as soon as his child shows the first signs of a curvature of the spine, he finds it reasonable that orthopaedic treatment should be carried on over several years, the difference in his behaviour is due to the better knowledge on the part of the physicians who pass on their knowledge honestly to the layman. Honesty on the part of the physician and willing acquiescence on the part of the layman will be established for the neuroses too, as soon as an insight into the nature of those affections becomes common property in the medical world. Radical treatment of these disorders will no doubt always require special training and will be incompatible with other kinds of medical activity. On the other hand, this class of physicians, which will, I believe, be a large one in the future, has the prospect of achieving noteworthy results and of obtaining a satisfying insight into the mental life of mankind.